The Hard Work of Happiness:
50 Life Lessons

RL Collins

DEDICATION

I dedicate this book to my family and friends who support me no matter what. I also dedicate this book to the haters who are against me no matter what. Life is a test, then you get the lesson.

Other books by RL Collins

Paranormal Romance & Suspense

Blood Magic

Blood Drops on the Virginia Trail: A Novel

Motivational & Self-Help

The Life and Times of Indigo Stone: 50 Life Lessons

Whispered Secrets in the Man Cave: 50 Life Lessons

The Hard Work of Happiness

Contents

ACKNOWLEDGMENTS

I have sincere gratitude for the people in my life who knowingly and unknowingly gave me the inspiration to write this book. In the past year, I have had high highs and low lows, but the ability to write about my experiences has helped me persevere.

SPRING

You leave old habits behind by starting out with the thought, "I release the need for this in my life".

–Wayne Dyer

1: Break the Loop of Negative Thinking

The most important relationship in your life is between you and you. There are many things in life that are outside your control such as politics, the economy, climate change, even the rude neighbor next door. But there are ways to tame your inner world and reduce obsessive negative thinking.

Everyone has a tone to their thoughts. The exact details of negative thinking are unique to everyone. However, once you are trapped in the loops it can be difficult to get out. So, what can you do?

The first thing to do is to accept that who you are at this moment is perfect. Develop loving kindness and compassion for yourself. You are not your thoughts. But your thoughts have power. It is your task to discover how to interrupt these thoughts because they take you out of your power.

One way to break obsessive thinking is to bring yourself to the present moment. Train yourself to become aware of your breath. You cannot breathe in and predict the future. You cannot breathe out and change the past. However, sitting in the present moment through at least one inhale and one exhale breaks the loop of negative thinking. This lasts if you can maintain your awareness of your breath.

Try this exercise. Focus on the tip of your nose. Travel up the bridge of your nose. Circle your right nostril. Circle your left nostril. Breathe in. How is the temperature of the air as you breathe in? Breathe out. How is the temperature of the air as you breathe out? Breathe in. How does breath travel down into your body? How far does it travel? To your chest? To your diaphragm? Down in your belly? Breathe out. Feel your body. Do you feel any restrictions to exhale? How can you push through the blocks to release the breath and take in fresh air?

Practice this for a few cycles. Then reflect. How do you feel? What percentage of your awareness is present? Anytime during your day when you feel your thoughts getting away from you, you can try this breath exercise. The goal is not to take a break for 5 minutes a day then go on with your life. The goal is to break the obsessive negative thinking and live a life of loving kindness, compassion, and presence.

Breathe. Let go. And remind yourself that this very moment is the only one you know you have for sure.

– Oprah Winfrey

2: Use Breathwork to Reduce Anxiety & Overthinking

Imagine the possibility of your breath being your soul or spirit. Your breath is sacred. Your breath is always communicating with you. It has something to say, to you. Your breath keeps you alive. Breath connects your inner world with your outer world and vice versus. When you see your breath in this light, you are ready for the journey. You are ready to welcome your breath home as a practice of self-love.

To reduce the mental and physical effects of anxiety and obsessive thinking, you can use breathwork. The goal is to return you to a natural breath pattern. The first step to recognize your current breath pattern. Trauma, anxiety, and stress can change your breath without you realizing it. The challenges of life can shorten your breath or make your breath shallow.

Try this practice to begin the journey to return to a more natural and healthy breath. You can do it standing, sitting, or lying down. Allow yourself to be as you are. Close your eyes.

Do a body scan. Feel your feet, legs, pelvis, belly, chest. Feel your hands, arms, shoulders. Feel your eyes, nose, mouth. Watch your next inhale. Feel the journey into your body. Feel the exhale leave your body. Study what you feel and imagine in the body. What do you think about your own natural breath pattern? Feel for where the breath likes to move. Feel where your body allows the breath to move. Notice where breath gets stuck. At the peak of your inhale, where does your body hold first?

Breathe in. Let your belly hang out. When you feel full, take in a little more air. Relax into the moment. Seek to discover the width of your breath. Exhale. On the next inhale, breathe wide into your ribs. See how wide you can breathe into your chest, 360 degrees. Breathe wide side to side, breathe wide back-to-back. Continue to soften your belly. Continue slowing down your breath. Focus on what is happening inside your body.

During the final phase bring it all together. Breathe in. Belly. Ribs. Chest. Collar bones. Cheeks bones. Eyes. Lips. In your own pace feel yourself fill up from the bottom to the top. Allow yourself to feel gratitude. Silently name anything you are grateful for and raise your vibration. At the end, allow your eyes to open. Say thank you. Come back another day and try again.

Stop walking through the world looking for confirmation that you don't belong. You will always find it because you've made that your mission.

— Brené Brown

3: Master the Inner Critic

The inner critic is the persistent inner voice that undermines your self-esteem and overall wellbeing. The inner critic can be relentless in making you feel less than and incapable of large and small accomplishments. Begin today to dissolve the inner critic and be the superhero in your life.

Journaling can help you break free from the chains of self-doubt. By putting pen to paper, you can unleash your thoughts and emotions. You externalize internal dialogue. You gain insight into your thoughts and behavior. Journaling cultivates self-awareness. Self-awareness is important because you learn to observe your thoughts and emotions without judgment. You become conscious of the recurring patterns and triggers. You can challenge the validity of the inner critic.

Journaling is a tool of self-reflection. You can revisit past events and situations and gain new insight. You can often go back into the past in a healthy way to change toxic patterns. You give yourself time and space to sit with your inner self that may not be available to you during the day.

Through journaling you can tap into your self-compassion and intuition. You gain access to wisdom and deeper insights. You learn to connect with yourself and make better decisions in work, love, life. Journaling makes you aware of your thoughts, emotions, and challenges. You develop a kind inner dialogue so you can show empathy towards yourself and others.

Journaling is a powerful tool that helps you break free of the inner critic. You can live a more authentic and happy life. By fostering a conscious and compassionate mindset, you find peace in life. You become strong enough to navigate the difficulties of life without crashing into the valley.

Self-care is not selfish. You cannot serve from an empty vessel.

— Eleanor Brownn

4: Put Yourself First & Feel Like a Winner

Putting yourself first helps you win at love, life, and work. Putting yourself first is not selfish. It is important to develop a routine of self-care that makes you strong in mind, body, and soul. Below are short points to remember as you take care of you in this hectic world.

Mind
- Discover what you want in life and a plan to obtain it.
- Cut distractions and do not sweat the small stuff.
- Accept failure as lessons.
- Discover your truth in life and your why's.
- Learn how to navigate toxic people and situations.

Body
- Learn basic nutrition and what is good for you to eat and drink.
- Add exercise and movement to your day every day.
- Get 7-9 hours of sleep each night and develop healthy sleep hygiene.
- Find strategies to maintain healthy teeth, skin, and hair.
- Everything in moderation.

Soul
- When times get tough, to whom do you turn? God? Therapist? Or a friend?
- During challenging times, how to you vent your frustration in a healthy way when no one is available?
- Always do the right thing even when nobody is watching. We have enough "crooks" trying to get ahead in life.
- As you strive to accomplish your goals in life, do no harm to others.
- During those times when your cup is full, how can you give back to others?

Taking care of your mind and thoughts helps you navigate the expected and unexpected in life. Taking care of your body helps you be in this world as a human being and be mobile and independent. Taking care of your soul or spirit or whatever you choose to call it; helps you maintain your values and beliefs and have good energy in world where many people are frazzled and/or wearing a mask. When you take care of yourself and have large and small wins, it also makes you a better partner whether it is a romantic, plutonic, or work relationship.

Tough times don't last but tough people do.

—Robert H. Schuller

5: Inspire Yourself to Do Your Body Right!

Treat your body right and your body will do right by you. Every day we are blasted with social media messages on what to eat and what to drink. How do you dig through and find a foundation to help you stand strong?

We often learn nutrition at home when we are children. Our diets can be affected by income, access to health education, and fitting in with our families and communities. However, after a while, you must educate yourself on the facts of nutrition. You can start simple with books from the local library, verified health websites, and documentaries on television. If you have the access, you can try a nutritionist through your healthcare plan, a personal trainer from the local gym, or a get fit program. Choose a method that works for you.

Protein
As you age, you naturally lose muscle and need to strength train and add more protein to your diet. The protein you eat helps you build muscle and recover from strenuous exercise. Protein helps with weight loss and satiety. There are free online calculators that will help you calculate the grams of protein needed based on your age, weight, and fitness goals.

Exercise
Once you leave your 20-30's you need more exercise to maintain fitness. With weight gain comes the risk of heart disease, diabetes, certain cancers, and more. Let's avoid or minimize this. It is also wise to change your fitness routine from time to time. Doing the same exercise routine gets too easy for our bodies that need a regular challenge. We need cardio, strength training, and stretching. Find something you enjoy doing and you will stick with it.

Whole Foods
Eat whole food! This is food grown straight from the Earth, plants, animals, etc. Much of the food you see advertised on T.V. is processed. Read the ingredients labels on some popular items you see in the grocery store. If you cannot pronounce it, it is probably processed. If it is boxed, canned, cooked then frozen, it is processed. Processed foods have extra sugar, salt, and fat. Avoid it.

Water
It is a myth that you need 8 glasses of water a day. Some people need more or less. Either way, drinking pure water is important. 70% of our bodies are made of water. Make is part of your daily routine to drink water. You can jazz it up with fruit.

You're off to great places! Today is your day! Your mountain is waiting, so get on your way!

— Dr. Seuss

6: Your Mountain is Waiting

Spring is a wonderful time for new beginnings. Often, we make New Year's resolutions, but sometimes it is easier to flow with the change of seasons. In the spring, the snow and ice melt. The flowers and trees are in bloom. Animals come of out hiding and frolic. Here are practical tips to create new healthy habits in a new season or whenever you choose to make positive changes.

1. Commit to Thirty Days
Three to four weeks is all the time you need to make a habit automatic. If you can make it through the initial conditioning phase, it becomes much easier to sustain. A month is a good block of time to commit to a change since it easily fits in with your calendar.

2. Make it Daily
Consistency is critical if you want to make a habit stick. If you want to start exercising, go to the gym every day for your first thirty days. Going a couple of times, a week will make it harder to form the habit. Activities you do once every few days are trickier to lock in as habits.

3. Start Simple
Don't try to completely change your life in one day. It is easy to get over-motivated and take on too much. If you want to study two hours a day, first make the habit of going for thirty minutes and build on that.

4. Remind Yourself
Around two weeks into your commitment it can be easy to forget. Place reminders to execute your habit each day or you might miss a few days. If you miss time, it defeats the purpose of setting a habit to begin with.

5. Stay Consistent
The more consistent your habit the easier it will be to stick. If you want to start exercising, try going at the same time, to the same place for your thirty days. When cues like time of day, place and circumstances are the same in each case it is easier to stick.

Take a good look at your life and how to make tweaks here and there. You can start with small changes. Think about what would make you the best version of yourself? Is there something you always wanted to try or work on? Sit in stillness until the answer comes to you. Then make your plan. Write it down. Put it on a post it. Whatever works for you. Then take the first step to climb the mountain to a better version of yourself.

What seems impossible today will one day become your warm-up.

—Unknown

7: New Habits in a New Season!

With all the social media, we all know the benefits of exercise. Most experts say we need 30 minutes of exercise each day or we need 150 minutes per week. For exercise to be effective, however, you must get your heart rate up and sweat. You must challenge yourself and reach beyond your daily comfort zone. In addition to a set time for exercise, you need movement throughout the day. Sitting for 5 hours or more daily is as detrimental to your health as being a chain smoker. Walk up the stairs at work instead of taking the elevator. Rake the leaves in the fall instead of paying the local youth to do it. Use the family pet as an excuse to play for 10 minutes and walk and dance around the house.

It is crucial that you get 7-9 hours of sleep each night. Our bodies and minds rejuvenate during sleep. Without hitting reset though a good night's sleep—toxins, stress, and anxieties build up until we are sick in large and small ways. Developing good sleep hygiene is finding what helps relax you and puts you to sleep.

A good sleep routine could include the following:
- meditation,
- quiet reading,
- light music,
- a warm bath,
- or a sound machine.

Regulate the temperature in your bedroom. Most people have the best sleep at 68 degrees. Treat your body right and your body will do right by you. Start small and adjust your routine to improve your self-care.

If you are not sure how to get started, try a professional such as…
- a nutritionist,
- personal trainer,
- primary care doctor,
- or a reputable website such as the Mayo Clinic.

As we age, it is important to manage sleep, diet, and exercise. These are the main pillars of good health. A lot of health knowledge is free, but practice discernment and watch out for fake news.

When these three pillars are strong, you can mentally and physically navigate the ups and downs of life. Start today to educate yourself on what you need for your age, weight, gender, etc. and make a plan to do better.

Stand tall; your strength is your voice.

—Unknown

8: Assertive Communication: Three-Part Series

Welcome to a three-part series on assertive communication. No matter the time of year, it is never too late to for new positive beginnings. Start with how you communicate with others. Build bridges and find the support you need to persevere through the expected and unexpected.

Let's begin by defining assertive communication…

Assertive Communication: A communication style in which a person stands up for their own needs and wants, while also taking into consideration the needs and wants of others, without behaving passively or aggressively.

Traits of Assertive Communicators

- Clearly state needs and wants
- Eye contact
- Listens to others without interruption
- Appropriate speaking volume
- Steady tone of voice
- Confident body language

Assertiveness Tips

Respect yourself. Your needs, wants, and rights are as important as anyone else's. It's fine to express what you want, so long as you are respectful toward the rights of others.

Express your thoughts and feelings calmly. Giving the silent treatment, yelling, threatening, and shaming are all fitting examples of what not to do. Take responsibility for your emotions and express them in a calm and factual manner. Try starting sentences with "I feel…"

Plan what you're going to say. Know your wants and needs, and how you can express them, before entering a conversation. Produce specific sentences and words you can use.

Say "no" when you need to. You can't make everyone happy all the time. When you need to say "no," do so clearly, without lying about the reason. Offer to help find another solution.

Save these tips. Review the tips. It will take time and practice to understand and effectively use assertive communication strategies. Believe in yourself.

Stand before the people you fear and speak your mind - even if your voice shakes.

—Maggie Kuhn

9: Assertive Communication: Part Two on Self-Advocacy

Welcome to part two of a three-part series on assertive communication. It is time for new positive beginnings. Start with how you communicate with others. Build bridges and find the support you need to persevere through the expected and unexpected.

Last post, we defined assertive communication. This post, we dig deeper. We all need to know how to positively communicate our needs. However, do you understand your needs? Have you defined what matters most to you? Let's dig into the concept of self-advocacy.

What is self-advocacy?
Self-advocacy is the ability to speak up on your behalf effectively. You might do this to bring about positive results in any of the various contexts in which you interact — whether at work, in organizations, school, community, or family.

Understanding yourself, your values, and your needs
Self-advocacy requires that you first understand yourself (your values, your needs, and your rights) in the context in which you live life. It requires that you be aware of the support that you need and the resources that are available professionally and personally.

Self-advocacy also requires the ability to communicate your value, your needs, and your human rights in a way that will be understood and offer you the greatest return on the ask.

To understand who you are, ask the following questions:

- What are my values?
- What matters to me most and why?
- What are my needs? What do I need to accomplish my tasks or fulfill my responsibilities? What do I need to feel respected and to maintain my emotional, physical, and financial well-being?
- What are my strengths and growth areas?

Understanding your context
Second, you need to understand yourself in the context of your role within the larger group. This means having a good understanding of the family, school, community, or organization's values, rules, rights, and resources. For instance, look at your family and the role you play in keeping the group productive and healthy. Or look at your place of employment and your role in fulfilling the professional vision and mission. Consider jotting down a list or journaling what

comes to mind.

The most common way people give up their power is by thinking they don't have any.

— Alice Walker

10: Assertive Communication: The 3 Communication Styles

Welcome to the final installment of the three-part series on assertive communication. In the first post, we defined assertive communication. In the second post, we helped you clearly define your needs and wants that need to be communicated. In this final post, we are comparing assertive communication to passive and aggressive so you can avoid the pitfalls and recognize the red flags in others.

Passive Communication
During passive communication, a person prioritizes the needs, wants, and feelings of others, even at their own expense. The person does not express their own needs or does not stand up for them. This can lead to being taken advantage of, even by well-meaning people who are unaware of the passive communicator's needs and wants.

· Soft spoken / quiet · Allows others to take advantage · Prioritizes needs of others · Poor eye contact / looks down or away · Does not express one's own needs or wants · Lack of confidence

Aggressive Communication
Through aggressive communication, a person expresses only their own needs, wants, and feelings matter. The other person is bullied, and their needs are ignored.

· Easily frustrated · Speaks in a loud or overbearing way · Unwilling to compromise · Use of criticism, humiliation, and domination · Frequently interrupts or does not listen · Disrespectful toward others

Assertive Communication
Assertive communication emphasizes the importance of both people's needs. During assertive communication, a person stands up for their own needs, wants, and feelings, but also listens to and respects the needs of others. Assertive communication is defined by confidence, and a willingness to compromise.

· Listens without interruption · Clearly states needs and wants · Willing to compromise · Stands up for own rights · Confident tone / body language · Good eye contact

You can start today by practicing these tips and suggestions to be a great communicator and live a life of win-win situations with family, friends, and co-workers.

Most people do not listen with the intent to understand; they listen with the intent to reply.

— Stephen Covey

11: Listen to Understand

In this life we have a lot of people "talking" to us at home, at work, in the grocery store, and more. But are we really listening? Active listening, listening to understanding, is an art developed over time. The benefit to active listening is better relationships in love, life, and work. With great listening skills, it is easier to resolve misunderstandings instead of sitting in conflict over a period of time. Start today and take the first step to be a better listener and friend to those who matter in your world.

What is active listening?
Active listening is treating listening as an active process, rather than a passive one. This means participating in conversation, rather than acting as an audience. Active listeners show they are listening, encourage sharing, and strive to understand the speaker. Show you're listening and put away distractions. Watching TV, using your phone, or doing other things while listening sends the message that your person's words are not important. Putting away distractions allows you to focus on the conversation and help a friend feel heard.

Use verbal and nonverbal communication.
Body language and short verbal cues that match the speaker's affect (e.g., responding excitedly if the speaker is excited) show interest and empathy. Verbal: "mm-hmm" / "uh-huh" "that's interesting" "that makes sense" "I understand." Nonverbal communication is nodding in agreement, reacting to emotional content (e.g., smiling) and making eye contact. Encourage sharing by asking open-ended questions. These are questions that encourage elaboration, rather than "yes" or "no" responses. Open-ended questions tell those in your world that you are listening, and you want to learn more.

Examples of active listening.
"What is it like to ____?" "How did you feel when ____?" "Can you tell me more about ____?" "How do you ____?" "What do you like about ____?" "What are your thoughts about ____?"

Use reflections.
In your own words, summarize the other person's most important points. Be sure to include emotional content, even if it was only communicated through tone or body language.

Friend: I've been having a tough time at work. There's way too much to do and I can't keep up. My boss is frustrated that everything isn't done, but I can't help it.
You: It sounds like you're doing your best to keep up, but there's too much work. That sounds stressful!

Where there is love there is life.

–Mahatma Gandhi

12: Love: How to Fight Fair

Love is love. Miscommunication happens every now and then and it is normal. Do not lose great love because of an inability to resolve small conflict respectfully. Learn how to fight fair.

How do you learn to fight fair?

Before you begin, ask yourself why you feel upset. Are you angry because your partner left the mustard on the counter? Or are you angry because you feel like you're doing an uneven share of the housework, and this is just one more piece of evidence? Take time to think about your own feelings before starting an argument.

Discuss one topic at a time.

Don't let "You left dishes in the sink" turn into "You watch too much TV." Discussions that get off-topic are more likely to get heated, and less likely to solve the original problem. Choose one topic and stick to it. No degrading language. Discuss the issue, not the person. No put-downs, swearing, or name-calling. Degrading language is an attempt to express negative feelings while making sure your partner feels just as bad. Doing so leads to more character attacks while the original issue is forgotten.

Express your feelings with words.

"I feel hurt when you ignore my phone calls." "I feel scared when you yell." Structure your sentences as "I" statements ("I feel emotion when event") to express how you feel while taking responsibility for your emotions. However, starting with "I" does not give a license to ignore the other fair fighting rules.
Take turns speaking. Give your full attention while your partner speaks. Avoid making corrections or thinking about what you want to say. Your only job is to understand their point of view, even if you disagree. If you find it difficult not to interrupt, try setting a timer allowing 1-2 minutes for each person to speak without interruption.

No stonewalling.

Sometimes, the easiest way to respond to an argument is to retreat into your shell and refuse to speak. This is called stonewalling. You might feel better temporarily, but the original issue will remain unresolved, and your partner will feel more upset. If you absolutely cannot go on, tell your partner you need to take a time-out. Agree to resume the discussion later.

To let go does not mean to get rid of.
To let go means to let be. When we
let be with compassion, things come
and go on their own,

–Jack Kornfield

13: Spring Forward & Let Go of Control

Spring is here! Use this change in season to change your perspective on life. Spring forward into positivity and let go of an unhealthy need to control. Letting go is more of an art than a science.

You can learn skills to support your transitions through change and uncertainty. These practices support you in knowing what to hold on to and what to let go of. Here are some tips from *Better Up Blog*.

1. Focus on what you can control

You can't control external events or others' reactions. You only have control over your mindset, attitudes, responses, and reactions.

You need to learn to trust that the things that are out of your control will happen as they do and will work out for the best.

There are a few different ways to build this trust, and different methods work for everyone. For some, religious faith helps them relinquish control. Others put their trust in the universe or fate.

Others have learned from experience that most things out of their control tend to resolve themselves positively. They may decide to put their trust in pure statistical evidence.

Do what works for you.

2. Don't rush through the transition

Fully embrace endings and name your losses (even if they are failures). Think about what to hold lightly, what to hold tightly and what to let go of that no longer serves you.

Practice letting go of a stated outcome and instead allow options and possibilities to enter your mind. This is where your new beginning might form right in front of your eyes.

3. Be in reality

You may not like the change around you but ignoring it won't change it or support you in managing through the transition.

Adopt a mindset that fully acknowledges the new reality. Don't ask yourself how you can change it back.

Instead, ask yourself: "Now that this has happened, how will I respond?"

4. Identify your triggers

Identifying the triggers that make you want to control external events gives you information. You can then use interventions to disrupt your thought process and shift your mindset.

Notice tension in your body or increases in anxiety responses.

This is a particularly useful technique for dealing with painful feelings related to trauma. It helps you to avoid a circumstance that might trigger a stress response.

Take action to relax and calm your body and your mind.

All that clutter used to be money.

–Joshua Becker

14: *Spring Has Sprung – Organize Your Life!*

Spring has sprung! Now is an exciting time to organize your life. Get rid of the old that no longer serves a purpose. Bring in the new that will help you excel in work, love, and life.

Here are 5 organizational skills and techniques from *Life Hack*.

1. MAKE A LIST

If you're feeling swamped with tasks, creating a to-do list is great for taking back control of the things you need to do.

By writing down your tasks in order of importance (make sure you prioritize your list!), you'll have a visualization of what needs to get done.

You'll also get to experience the feeling of great relief when you get to cross a task off your to-do list when it's completed!

2. DON'T RELY ON YOUR MEMORY

Even if you have superhuman memory, it's always a good idea to write everything down.

From project deadlines to customer details, to product prices, writing things down can serve as a reminder so you don't forget the important things when you're feeling overwhelmed.

And with most of us carrying around smartphones, you're never far from a tool where you can write something down.

3. SCHEDULE

A huge part of being organized is knowing how to plan, and expert planning involves a lot of scheduling.

Scheduling is taking a step further than creating a to-do list. Not only do you have the things you need to do recorded, but you have a timetable when you should complete them. This helps you to develop your time management skills as you're expected to coordinate tasks and activities so that deadlines are met and everything is done on time.

4. LEARN TO DELEGATE

Learning to delegate tasks is a valuable skill that will help to keep you organized. Not only will it lighten your workload, but it will sharpen your planning and prioritization skills as you will have to learn which tasks should be done by you and which tasks are okay to be given to someone else.

5. AVOID MULTITASKING

While the idea of attempting to do more than one task simultaneously may seem brilliant, in practice, it's the complete opposite. Multitasking is known to lower your productivity as it diminishes your focus and attention and things become more difficult and take longer to complete.

If this is new for you or you haven't shaken things up in this way for a long time, start small. Take baby steps and congratulate yourself on every bit of progress. If you make a mistake or misstep, do not worry. Come back another day and try again.

SUMMER

Be selective with your battles. Sometimes peace is better than being right.

– Tiny Buddha

15: Remove Difficult People from Your Life – Take the High Road

Difficult people are part of life. Whether you are at work, at home, or simply out in life, there is always that person who annoys you. How do you take the high road and avoid conflict? Why get involved with someone who lives for the fight? Here are three tips to help you take the high road:

1. Remind yourself that it is NOT about you!

We all tend to personalize our experiences in life. Take that coworker who walks past your desk every morning and never seems to acknowledge you, smile, say hello, or start a conversation. It is easy to assume this person is deliberately ignoring you and to take their affront personally. We will question why they say hello to one person and not to you and assume they are ignoring you deliberately.

They likely aren't ignoring you. They are probably a million miles inside their heads and aren't thinking about you, aren't thinking that you are taking this personally, and aren't trying to be rude either. They are just thinking about something else.

When you default to taking things personally, take a time-out and ask if there is another explanation that has nothing to do with you. Take the high road, and don't assume that their behavior is a personal attack. It likely isn't.

2. Learn to bite your tongue.

It is tempting to say what comes to mind in the heat of the situation, but it will cause tensions to rise rather than dissipate. Biting your tongue is an example of taking the high road. Don't say what is on the tip of your tongue. While it can be satisfying to snap back with a smart retort, it may be something you regret.

3. Respond vs. React.

When we react, we get caught up in the emotions of the situation. When we respond, we have thought through what we are going to say, why we are going to say it, and how we will say it. By taking that pause, we can avoid a situation that causes regret.

There are times when we do need to say things, but by choosing to wait, you can take the time to respond professionally and not emotionally. If you are going to have a conversation, give yourself a 24 hour wait before saying what you want to say. Your emotions will be calmer; you will be more professional; you will be taking the high road.

Taking the high road, being graceful, professional, and classy, is not accidental. It's intentional. Intentionally think about what you're going to say. Intentionally think about when you're going to say it. Intentionally remove yourself from personal feelings of what's going on. Intentionally be careful about what you're doing. Take that high road.

The simpler the space, the calmer the mind.

–Jennifer Noseworthy

16: Eclipse the Old and Organize Your Life

The summer slowdown is a suitable time to self-reflect and to set intentions for a positive productive life. Shed old skin and say hello to new beginnings. Start with organizing your life. When there are many things in our lives outside our control, it helps us to learn how to manage small things.

Let's continue…

6. MINIMIZE INTERRUPTIONS
It's impossible to control every aspect of your environment but it doesn't hurt to try. By minimizing interruptions while you're at work, it gives you a better chance of completing them as effectively and efficiently as possible.
Investing in noise-cancelling headphones or installing a social media block on your desktop are examples of ways you could reduce distractions.

7. REDUCE CLUTTER
A notable organizational skills training technique is to create a filing system for your documents. Whether it's at work or at home, we all accumulate documents that we may not currently need but are too afraid to throw away in case we will need it in the future.

8. ORGANIZE YOUR WORKSPACE
Where we work influences how we work. If you have a cluttered and messy workspace, then the chances of you working in an unorganized fashion can be very high.

Keeping an organized workspace ensures that you're able to perform at your most productive. You won't waste time looking for things that have been misplaced and working in a clutter-free environment can be soothing for your mind.

9. GET RID OF WHAT YOU DON'T NEED
Clutter is known to lead to stress and anxiety. If you're already feeling overwhelmed, then the sight of clutter can increase that feeling.
Getting rid of things, you no longer need to clear out your environment and, hopefully, your mind as well.

Done with that sticky note? Throw it away! Inbox is filled to the brim with unread emails? Unsubscribe to newsletters you no longer read! Whatever you no longer require in your physical and digital life, get rid of it.

10. TIDY UP REGULARLY
While working, it can get easy for your desk to get untidy. You're focused on

work and so keeping everything at your desk in order is probably a lower priority. But it's something to be conscious of. Doing a regular tidy up can ensure the mess on your desk doesn't go overboard.

Whether it's a quick clean up every day, or a deep clean every month. Being aware of tidying up and fitting it into your routine will help keep you organized and less stressed.

Keep watering yourself. You're growing.

–E. Russell

17: Self-Love vs. Being Selfish

It is okay to take time for yourself. At times society can promote endless giving to prove you are a "good" person or worthy of recognition and acceptance by others. Loving yourself and putting yourself first in healthy ways, helps you stand strong in times of uncertainty.

So, what is true self-love? True self-love starts with acceptance of who you are today. You acknowledge your strengths and weaknesses as a human being. You know there are ways to be better in life for yourself, your family, even your employer, but it is not an emergency.

Genuine self-love is also taking simple measures to be happy and whole in life. Instead of spending years toiling away for that luxury car, have a second cup of coffee with rich, decadent hazelnut creamer. Instead of spending the month shopping for the perfect gift for your partner, order in one night, pull out a good bottle of wine, and your time and attention all evening is the best gift of all.

Self-love is also synonymous with self-compassion. You understand that whether you are having a good day or a difficult day, all you need to do in life is your best at that moment. Perfection is a fantasy and when you make a mistake, learn from it, have a course correction, and keep going. Loving yourself is also being able to stand in this world where we are fed negatives messages about our appearance, talents, and accomplishments. What really matters is what we think of ourselves.

When you love yourself, nobody can shake you! An angry, needy friend cannot make you have a bad week. A jealous co-worker cannot rain on your parade when you win an award. Someone stealing your favorite parking spot does not send you into a tiff. You navigate life with a positive sense of well-being even when you do not know what is around the next corner.

Start today and examine who you are in life. Acknowledge how far you have come. What are the small, simple pleasures you can do for yourself to have moments of joy? How can you let go of the need to be approved by people and situations outside of yourself?

Piglet noticed that even though he had a Very Small Heart, it could hold a rather large amount of Gratitude.

–A.A. Milne, "Winnie-the-Pooh"

18: Grateful, Thankful, Blessed!

Any time you turn on the news, there are 101 reasons to be afraid, depressed, and hopeless. There is an air of doom and gloom around the politics, inflation, and more. Having an attitude of gratitude is the best way to deflect the chaos in our world. Focus on what is going well in your life.

When you appreciate the small accomplishments in life, you attract more abundance. Thankfulness gives you the energy to persevere with goals. Gratitude helps you maintain a positive circle of friendship with others. Acknowledging your blessings keeps you open to new opportunities for growth and development.

So how to you learn to practice gratitude? It is remarkably simple. There are no fixed rules. And if someone tells you that you are doing it wrong, they are a Debbie Downer!

First, you can write down why you are grateful. You can write in a journal, gratitude app, post it, anything! Start small. If you woke up this morning without any aches and pains – be grateful. If you have healthy food in your refrigerator – be thankful. If you have clothes that keep you cool during hot summer weather – have gratitude.

Second, make it a habit to express your gratitude. Perhaps set aside five minutes at the end of each day to review positive experiences large and small. Perhaps when you have your lunch break, make a list of accomplishments from the morning. Perhaps when you brush your teeth in the morning, jot down small wins from the day before.

Lastly, keep your blessings private to you and select family or friends. The practice is for you to keep motivated in times of uncertainty. Unless you have a comrade taking the same gratitude journey, others may not understand or may have envy. Be your own best cheerleader. Navigate the Debbie Downers or those who may not understand that the glass really is half full. Stay on course!

grit

/grit/

noun

2. courage and resolve; strength of character.

19: The Gift of Grit

The dictionary definition of grit is having "courage, resolve, or a strength of character." The gift of grit is the ability to push through challenges when there is no guarantee of success. Many times, in life we have a blueprint or steps to follow that promise of obtaining goals. Surviving on grit is like being in the Artic wilderness with flint for fire and a compass to find your way back home. You just go for it and hope for the best!

The important thing about grit is that it has nothing to do with IQ points or wealth in life. Grit is a deep belief and trust in your ability to live life and survive no matter what. You may have family, friends, and co-workers that you believe will be there for you in tough times, but no matter what, you show up for you every time.

It takes time and countless failures to develop grit. There is no magic book or course to take to develop grit. You fall ninety-nine times and get back up on the 100th attempt. A few lucky ones may have parents or grandparents who model grit. Others may have health scares or experience a natural disaster early in life that develops grit. Others may be born with a disability that requires the need to build grit and live successfully in society. And then, there is always the power of prayer.

Whether you feel you have grit today or hope to develop it tomorrow, all you need to do is keep living life. Correct your course as you meet obstacles and challenges but keep moving forward. Never stop learning, growing, moving forward. Believe in the best possible outcome for yourself. When you are too tired to keep pushing, have a warm drink, and go to bed early. In the morning, use your renewed strength to continue.

Do not let the behavior of others destroy your inner peace.

– Dalai Lama

20: Learn How to Welcome Peace

You may think the title of this blog is very odd. Who needs to learn how to welcome peace? Isn't peace what everyone wants in their life? Well…

I'm sure we all know at least one person who is constantly whining, complaining, or an all-around Debbie Downer. Have you ever actually stopped for a moment to listen to what these individuals are upset about? Many times, they are upset about nothing, or the ordinary ups and downs of life. It is outside one's control.

This author has the experience of a friend who gets upset when the mail is late. Um, hello, it has been a few years since the huge publicity around cutting funds to the United States Post Office, the shortage of mail carriers during this pandemic, and more. Late mail? Yes, and? This author has the experience of a co-worker who gets upset when their healthcare agency updates their website to have the latest COVID booster but did not call every member on the telephone sharing the exact same information. Um, what? What agency has that kind of customer service today?

Yes, dear reader, some people need to learn how to welcome peace. Make sure you know how to welcome peace. Having the ability to welcome peace means you understand that life is not perfect, but you have obtained the most important wins in life. The most important wins in life might be food, shelter, clothing, and gas in your car or money for public transportation.

Depending on the social media you listen to, celebrities, politicians, community leaders make life more complicated than it must be. You can't just have a car; you must have the latest and greatest vehicle with built in Wi-fi and Sirius radio. You can't just have clothes and shoes that keep you warm; you must have a celebrity name brand or fabric weaved from plant fibers from a select farm.

Learn how to welcome peace and not focus on the small imperfect details of life. What are your top five priorities as a human being, partner, parent, friend, daughter/son, etc.? Sometimes, just sometimes, life is good. You can be happy and content, despite the little bumps in the road. Accept life. Embrace life. Be at peace.

To be yourself in a world that is constantly trying to make you something else is the greatest accomplishment.

– Ralph Waldo Emerson

21: Celebrating Your Differences and Uniqueness

At work, at home, and in our communities, people typically prefer the company of someone who looks like them, thinks like them, acts like them. What do you do when you are different and do not fit in with general society? Celebrate it!

Here is how....

Play to your strengths

What makes you different in the workplace might be an asset. Are you a super productive early bird when your co-workers are grumbling and not fully awake until lunchtime? Use it to your advantage to cross off your to-do list with superior work, be eligible for the next promotion, and beat the competition.

Plant yourself in a niche

Are you the dog whisperer? Do the neighborhood cats spend time together in your backyard? If you find that animals or children love your company, find a niche in life where you are loved. Consider volunteering at an animal shelter. Succeed with furry friends who might have high anxiety after being neglected, abandoned, or abused. Over time, turn the volunteer opportunity into a paid position where you are irreplaceable.

Develop self-confidence and independence

Accept your uniqueness and build unshakeable self-confidence. Learn to stand on your own two feet and not rely on people. What others criticize in you may be a talent they wish they had. Others may be uncomfortable with your stellar abilities.

Deflect the envy

Deflect envy. Believe it or not, our biggest enemy is often our biggest admirer. Be alert if you are in the workplace, at home, or in your own community and you have someone who is actively working against you. Unless you have wronged this person, their negative attitude is typically envy. This person may see the greatness in you that you may not acknowledge in yourself. Wherever you go in this world, be humble, watch what you say to other people, and always keep it positive. Envious people are quick to fly off the handle if they perceive one ounce of criticism from a uniquely talented person.

Tell the negative committee that meets inside your head to sit down and shut up.

– Ann Bradford

22: Seize the Moment! Let Go of Negative Self-Talk!

Seize the moment and let go of negative self-talk. Most negative self-talk is ruminating over the past, fearing the future, or internalizing the criticism of people in your circle. Learn to live in the moment and drop the limiting self-beliefs.

The past is done. The past cannot be changed. Ruminating over the past is wishing things were different or fear that the situation will return. When life disappoints you, feel what you feel, find the lesson, then move on! When you have concerns over the future, set positive intentions, take the necessary steps, then let go of the need to control the outcome. If you have someone in your inner circle constantly criticizing you, figure out if you really need this person by your side, how you can limit your time with this person, then set healthy boundaries.

When you learn to live in the moment, you drop worries over the past and future and you can just be! Another strategy to letting go of negative self-talk is to replace it with positive affirmations. Human beings have 50,000-80,000 thoughts a day. Thoughts cannot be stopped. But you can replace and retrain your mind to focus on the positive aspects of life.

Start small with five minutes a day and work your way up to 10, 15, 20, or more. Meditation is an option, and you can find free guided meditation online. Journaling is a wonderful tool. You can privately list all gripes and concerns without an audience and get it off your chest. The power of prayer is healthy no matter your religion. Ask for guidance, support from a higher power, and give up trying to micromanage people and situations outside your control. When all else fails, burn off the energy of negative self-talk by dancing, singing, or going for a long drive.

Letting go doesn't mean giving up but rather accepting that there are things that cannot be.

–Unknown

23: Knowing When to Let Go

In this life there are many messages about perseverance, determination, going the long haul and more. But sometimes, you also need to know when to let go of people and situations. There is a difference between fighting the good fight and endless knocking on a closed door.

When is it time to fight the good fight?

Know your priorities in life. Write them down if you can. The list should not be endless or be 101 impossible feats. Ten must-dos in a year are good, even narrowing things down to five priorities is even better. Then develop an action plan. What can you do every day, every week to accomplish the important goal? You'll have your good days and bad days when you must persevere. Along the way you should have large and small wins. The task should motivate you to be your best self. You may not have a large crowd cheering you on, but at least one person should know you about the journey you walk and support you.

When is it time to stop knocking on a closed door?

Then, there are those goals we set for ourselves where we push, and push, and push, but really, it is not for us. You are knocking on a closed door. If there is a goal you have in life, that makes you sad, angry, depressed, most days—it might not be for you. If you invest a lot of time, money, or energy, for months, and years, and you get nowhere, it might not be for you. If the people you surround yourself with to accomplish the task are always working against you with endless conflict—it might not be for you.

The fine line...

It is an important life lesson to know when to persevere through challenges to accomplish remarkable things and when you are knocking on a closed door. At times, doors are closed to us, because there is something bigger, and better, for us to set our sights on. Be patient with yourself as you learn the difference and maintain the courage to reach for the stars.

I will not let anyone walk through my mind with their dirty feet.

– Ghandi

24: Dirty Feet & the Opinion of Others

Did you see what she is wearing? How much money did he make on that job? What did she say at the grocery store? I can't believe he is talking to that one.

Everybody, believe me, everybody has an opinion on what you say and do in this life. Some will even tell you to your face how they approve or disapprove of your adult choices. Others will whisper behind your back whether they perceive you to be a success or failure on life's stage.

The main thing to know is often our biggest critics are unhappy in their own lives, and misery loves company. Or our biggest critics are envious and jealous that we have large and small successes. The Ghandi quote means do not focus on the haters. Do not focus on people who are constantly negative.

The only person we have control over in this life is ourselves. You have 50,000-80,000 thoughts every day. There is no way to stop thinking. It is simply impossible. What you can do is redirect unwanted thoughts and opinions from others into positive messaging. Feed your mind love, encouragement, and motivation every day. This may be done through prayer, mantras, meditation, YouTube videos, songs, affirmations in front of the mirror, and more. Be your own best cheerleader!

At times you may even need to distance yourself from a Debbie Downer. Limit the phone calls. Limit the emails. Limit the happy hour gatherings. It is important to have healthy boundaries around people who are constantly negative and intrusive with their unwanted opinions. Life is too short to be bogged down in the opinions of others. Haters can distract you from having a healthy and positive enjoyment of life. The most valuable opinion is your own. You decide whether you will have a good day or a challenging day.

Don't underestimate the value of Doing Nothing, of just going along, listening to all the things you can't hear, and not bothering.

— Pooh's Little Instruction Book

25: The Art of Doing Nothing

We live in a "go hard or go home" culture. The art of doing nothing must be honed over time. Not everyone can do it right away. But it is a worthwhile skill to develop.

When you are always on the go, you miss opportunities for peace and self-reflection. It is in those quiet moments when you experience life's truths. Your partner's request for a new take-out restaurant was really about the need to get out of a rut. Your friend's quiet hellos and tired eyes are about the personal struggle he or she is dealing with. You realize you fill every minute of the hour with an activity because you do not want to feel loneliness.

Sitting alone in your own space also helps hone intuition. Intuition can be defined in many ways. It is the ability to read between the lines. Intuition gathers important unspoken information.

So, how do you learn the art of doing nothing? You can start small with five minutes a day. Use the time to meditate, do breath work, stretch, journal, or listen to music. Eventually, in weeks, months, or years, you will have the ability to sit in silence and just be.

FALL

Watch your thoughts, they become words; watch your words, they become actions; watch your actions, they become habits; watch your habits, they become character; watch your character, for it becomes your destiny.

–Frank Outlaw

26: Positive Communication through Difficult Emotions

We all have those days where life gets the best of us, and we are simply ticked off by a person or a situation. Navigating different personalities at home, at work, and in the community is part of life. Knowing how to have positive communication to resolve issues is golden.

The best thing to do when someone has angered you is to take a step back to regain your composure. Many bridges have been burned by saying something in the heat of the moment that you cannot take back. Unless it is a matter of life or death, give yourself time to calm down before addressing a person or situation that has angered you. You may need a whole 24 hours to do this. But do not let the anger sit. Do not let an issue sit and remain unresolved for weeks, months, or even years. Holding unspoken grudges is unhealthy mentally and physically. It is also unfair to the other person who may sense the tension but does not know the cause of it.

After you regain your composure, decide whether the issue is an ongoing problem or the other person simply having a difficult day. Once again, do not let ongoing issues fester. If you wish to maintain the relationship, it is always helpful to begin with "are you okay?" before assuming the other person offended you with real intent.

Many times, loved ones are distracted by tricky situations that have nothing to do with us, but they act out in ways that negatively affect other people. Once it is clear there is a specific problem, address it. What inspired the actions of the other person? How and why did it trigger you? How can you both work together to avoid conflict in the future? Keep in mind a realistic and fair solution for both parties.

Once the air has cleared, drop it, and do whatever it takes to maintain the peace. Real relationships need time and forgiveness. Miscommunication and misunderstandings are normal and part of life. The key is to resolve issues in a compassionate way so every is free to be human.

Rivers know this: there is no hurry.
We shall get there some day.

– A.A. Milne.

27: Using Patience to Achieve Your Dreams

I want. You want. We want. As children we are often told to be patient until whatever we desire arrives at the right time. Youth and being impulsive go hand in hand. As adults, we often just put more strength into the push to grab whatever we want in life. However, patience, real patience is a gift we give ourselves that is timeless.

The ability to wait for the right time to receive what we hold dear is made easier when we can occupy our mind with other worthwhile activities. Perhaps one day you wish to be married or have a life partner. Sure, you could download all the latest dating apps. Coordinate outfits to the local happy hours. Or even take your dog to the local park to force an air of being approachable with your cute pooch. But some things cannot be forced. You might get a date fast, but the best life partner will take time.

While you are waiting to land the promotion of your dreams in the workplace, you can invest your time into achieving smaller goals. How about taking a community college class on public speaking to keep your job skills sharp? How about coordinating family and friends to donate gently used clothes, including business clothes, to the local Goodwill center? How about teaching computer skills to senior citizens at your neighborhood library? Slow down and enjoy the journey to achieve important life goals.

It is easy to spin ourselves into circles trying to outsmart people and situations we think we have control over. The only person we have control over in this life, is ourselves. Anything you wish to achieve that relies on the cooperation of other people, institutions, or even biology, will simply take time. Be calm, cool, and collected. Keep your eyes on the prize. Invest in worthwhile dreams. But along the way pause and enjoy life.

Talk to yourself as you would someone you love.

– Brene Brown

28: Meet Yourself Where You Are

It is normal to experience ups and downs in life. We typically have plans to accomplish goals large and small. Sometimes we succeed. Sometimes we fail. Meeting yourself where you are is walking the path, enjoying the path, before you arrive at the destination.

The path

What is your goal for today? Getting to work on time? Buy groceries for the household? Repair the leaking sink? What is your goal for the week? The next month? It is normal for adults to have daily, weekly, and monthly goals. We strive to succeed in large and small ways. We beat ourselves up if we take a misstep or fall short. The best thing to do is to set out on a path that brings pride, peace, and inspires you to persevere. The end is not the goal or highlight of your existence. It is being true to yourself and committing to enrichment of your life.

The walking

Today's news outlets, social media, movies, music, etc. can have us feeling like bigger is better. As we live this life of ups and downs, we must be glammed up, well spoken, wearing gold thread in our clothes and more. But really, much of life is a private walk. Some shout their life experiences from the rooftops. While others keep their thoughts private in a journal. It all depends on the person. Meeting yourself where you are is understanding that you are not required to advertise, compare, or compete with the people around you. Your walk is not better or worse than the next person's. The walk is your unique experience of life.

The destination

If you do not enjoy the process of striving toward a particular goal, the thrill of achievement will be very brief. You might feel the high for a few minutes, few hours, maybe a full day. Then, it is time to find another flag to plant on the mountain top. It is a mark of maturity to take pride in working towards a goal. Find steps to take that bring peace and joy on a daily, weekly basis. Learn to celebrate small wins. Reaching your destination is great, but unless you are at the end of a well-lived life, there is more to come. Look forward to that "more."

If you are offended by my boundaries, then you are probably one of the reasons I need them.

–Unknown

29: *Healthy Boundaries, Get Some!*

Isn't she sweet? Isn't he kind? What a lady. What a good man. Yes, you can be all things great and good, but you better get some healthy boundaries with the people you meet out in society. The takers have no boundaries.

The myth to all the positivity thinking and coaching is that is makes you look weak or soft. This is not true. Having a positive mindset takes work and commitment. The right attitude carries you through the ups and downs of life without having you linger too long in the dark pits. You can love yourself and take care of family and friends. However, you must, must have healthy boundaries!

People who walk in the light are easy targets for the miserable, self-destructive, and downright mean personalities that live in this world generation after generation. Having healthy boundaries means knowing when to say "no" to someone who is not good for you. It means saying "no" to someone who always takes from you and never gives anything in return. It means saying "no" to someone who simply has not earned your trust.

People who are on your level will understand your healthy boundaries. The ones who cry foul and try to assassinate your character for saying "no" to this and that, are typically the users. These energy vampires are angry because they do not have access to your positive energy. Remember, the takers have no boundaries. It is up to you to keep your relationships positive and respectful and know when to shield yourself from the users.

If you ever get a second chance in life for something, you've got to go all the way.

–Lance Armstrong

30: Resurrection: Believe in Second Chances

When life gives you a second chance, take it. A specific person may not give you a second chance, but we are often presented with the same life lesson until we get it right.

This is a wonderful time to remember what is means to be human and live in a society that is often quick to misjudge and misunderstand people who are different. The differences can be based on skin color, hair style, preferred clothing, or something as deep as different political views and the institution of marriage.

We have no control over how others perceive us. Often a person's perception of you has nothing to do with you as a person but everything to do with the lens used to view the world. If you have a disagreement with someone, and he or she chooses to end the relationship – let it go and move on. However, consider how to present yourself differently next time. Look forward to the second chance.

Sixty percent of communication is nonverbal. People are less afraid or offended when what makes you unique is not a surprise. Now, you may not need to tattoo anything on your forehead or dress in eccentric clothes. But if you are a private sensitive person, do not walk around being overly friendly to strangers inviting them into your world. If you are a social butterfly and being around people energizes you, do not invest time in a quiet club or knitting or chess.

People today often cannot stand to hear an opinion with which they do not agree. But there are things you can do to make your personality stand out without a single word. Eventually, your real tribe will be able to spot you across the room. You'll find your niche where you can be you and shine like a star. When life gives you a second chance, take it.

Self-pity is our worst enemy and if we yield to it, we can never do anything wise in this world...

–Helen Keller

31: Stop the Pity Party – Ack!

Everyone has challenges and obstacles in their life. Family and friends may or may not understand you or be able to support you. Sometimes the person closest to you is the source of conflict. How do you stop the pity party when life feels out of control?

Nothing is permanent except death

Nothing in this life is permanent except death. Whatever tricky situation you are in, will pass. It may not pass as soon as you want it to, but it will pass. Grit your teeth and sit in them. Practice great self-care while you are in the storm. Good self-care includes managing your sleep, diet, and exercise.

Identify what is and is not within your control

Sh*t happens. No matter how often you pray, meditate, journal, etc. you cannot avoid life's challenges. You just learn to ride it out without falling apart. Many challenges we deal with in life are outside of our control. Difficult boss. Difficult co-workers. Critical mother-in-law. Global conflict that makes gas prices soar. What you do have control over is how you allow external forces affect your emotions. You have great control over your perception of the world and how you manage negative messages. You can choose to see the glass as half full or half empty.

Be your own cheerleader until times improve

A few people are incredibly lucky and grew up in perfect families and have wonderful friends who are always there for us. The rest of us come from families that had some sort of dysfunction. Friends get busy with work, love, and life. You must be your own cheerleader. Find ways to motivate yourself and encourage yourself to persevere through the difficulties of life. This is a commitment you make every day not just when times are tough. You can motivate yourself with inspirational videos, podcasts, quotes, mantras, prayers, and more. Build an armor of courage, determination, and self-love before you leave home every day.

When life feels out of control and you find yourself having a pity party, give it 24 hours, then take steps to turn things around.

Be thankful for all the difficult people in your life and learn from them. They have shown you exactly who you do not want to be.

–Unknown

32: How to Manage Difficult People

Whether it is work, love, or life, we all come across difficult people from time to time. How do you manage the snarky co-worker? How do you manage the competitive neighbor? How do you manage the person who wants to be your fiend to be in your business? Read on and find out...

Have great self-care

In this life the only person we have control over is ourselves. You have no control over the difficult men, women, and some children you meet in life. Everyday practice great self-care so you have the emotional resources to weather the storm. This includes a healthy routine for sleep, diet, and exercise. Depending on your faith it may include prayer, meditation, and journaling. You do whatever it takes to wrap yourself in the armor of self-love to face the world.

Set healthy boundaries

Takers have no boundaries. Difficult people often monopolize your time and attention for their own selfish purposes. It is up to you to decide what you will and will not allow in your world. If you know the after work happy hour is spent gossiping about the boss who supports you, are you going to go? If you know that by joining a popular club you must deal with a "playground" bully, do you really need the fame? If you know the restaurant with the impressive food has rude customer service, are you really going to spend your dollars there? Decide what is and is not worth your time.

Practice forgiveness

Not everybody comes from a great family. Not everybody learns from their mistakes in life and strive to be a better man or woman. Some people sit in chaos and dysfunction until the day they die, or they land in the retirement home. Be willing to forgive others for their misfortune and let go of the burden. Forgiveness does not mean you accept or condone their behavior. It means you see it for what it is, it is outside of your control, and you let go of it. Do not carry burdens of others on your back.

With a routine of great self-care, healthy boundaries, and the power of forgiveness you can navigate around the difficult people with grace and dignity.

Change is inevitable. Growth is optional.

–John C. Maxwell

33: Accepting Unexpected Change

We have been rolling through unexpected change for some time. Whether it was the COVID shut down, the need for reform in law enforcement, or overturning 50-year-old Supreme Court ruling—change is inevitable. The way to survive is to grow through it.

Know who you and what you will and will not stand for. For example, are you going to join that co-worker is destructive gossip to have a friend? Or will you go your own way and have private success?

What values and beliefs serve you well and what can be cut for a better life? For example, is it necessary to push and compete with everybody for what you want in life? Or can you simply strive to create a better version of yourself and attract abundance?

Understand what is a need and what is a want. For example, do you go to work every day for material gain to support your family? Or are you there for ego gratification such as cliques and pretty awards?

Once you get it down in your soul who you are through unexpected change, you need to decide how you will express yourself in a world of diverse personalities and life experiences. Decide what is a private matter and when to act. Are you navigating a community where differences can be celebrated? Or are you in a system where different is bad? Some of these questions are difficult to answer but necessary. Change is inevitable. Growth is optional.

Remind yourself: If it was easy, everyone would do it.

–Unknown

34: Personal Motivation: Sink or Swim

Depending on the season, depending on the year there are 101 gimmicks around personal motivation. Get a leadership coach. Try this communication class. Watch this podcast series. Buy the latest and greatest self-help book in personal empowerment. Despite the tool or strategy, the ability to motivate yourself through the ups and downs of life determines whether you sink or swim.

As children, we look to our parents to motivate and encourage us to succeed. Some do, some don't. As we get older, we look to our peers and teachers to motivate and encourage us to do our best. Some do, some don't. Once you become a full-fledged adult, it is up to you to discover what makes you feel like the hero in your own life.

If you are completely clueless, then yes, get a professional. Try the life coach. Try the rock star therapist. Try the communication class at the community college. But after a while, it is up to you to find a daily practice that allows you to wear an armor of positivity. It is critical to have tools that help you persevere in this unpredictable world.

It is important to be your own cheerleader because the people around you have their own lives to live. A spouse can jump in and help you every now and then. A friend can put down her daily to do list and give you a pep talk every now and then. A co-worker can stop by your cubicle to listen and give advice every and now and then. However, the only person responsible for your happiness is you.

In critical moments when tough decisions need to be made, rely on yourself. Use your logic and intuition to decide to say yes to that job, buy that house, or secure the investment. You can always put things on hold to ask another person, but unless the decision affects a group of people, part of being an adult is making tough decisions.

Personal motivation is accepting yourself flaws and all. It means knowing that sometimes you will make mistakes, learn the lesson, and try again. Personal motivation is understanding change is inevitable, but growth is optional. Self-empowerment is standing strong even though others may not understand or agree with you. It is up to you to find the best arena where you shine. Curate a menu of practices that help you have the confidence to surf the waves of life. If it is the podcast, self-help book, mantras, gratitude journals, etc. then go for it.

Simply wait, be quiet, be still. The world will freely offer itself to you.

–Franz Kafka

35: Wait, the Answers are in Stillness

As soon as we wake up, we are on our phones, scrolling through social media, turning on the stream TV. On the way to work we listen to the radio for road delays, or listen to speed traps on Waze, or even navigating the honking horns of impatient drivers. Throughout the noise, we are trying to solve the problem. We wonder how to get that promotion, how to find an effective fitness routine, where to find the best deals on expensive groceries, or the best way to navigate the politics in our community. After a certain point, when you decide to turn everything off, you find the answers by sitting in stillness.

It is important to find time in your day or your week to disconnect from life's distractions. In the quiet, you reconnect with who you are and what you need to be satisfied in this world. The quiet time might be the first thing in the morning, before sunrise. The quiet time might be late in the evening when the family is tucked into bed. You might even find time for stillness while parked in your car before entering the building for work, home, or the grocery store.

The "noise" of life coming from family, friends, co-workers, etc. is constantly sending us messages requiring us to do that or do this. It is extremely hard to make confident, successful life decisions when you are pulled in many directions. So sometimes, you just do you and sit for a moment.

The first time you sit in the stillness, do not expect a big epiphany. Enjoy being present. Breathe in. Breathe out. Give your attention to a favorite photograph. Hold a precious heirloom like a family necklace or bracelet. People watch from inside a window. Appreciate having a moment to do absolutely nothing.

Over time the answers come. Why does that co-worker irritate you so much? How she reminds you of the school yard bully from elementary school. Why do you spend so much on retail therapy buying brand new books? You really want to author your own original tales. Why do you spend so much time always saying "yes" to tedious favors for family, friends, and co-workers? You remember the times when you were alone in the world and wish someone would help you.

Starting today, decide to make time for the healthy habit of sitting in stillness at least once a day or a few times a week. Find the solutions to your most frustrating problems by sitting with the real you.

WINTER

Love yourself first, and everything else falls into line. You really have to love yourself to get anything done in this world...

– Lucille Ball

36: Self-Love: Set Internal Boundaries (Part 1)

Too often we look at family, friends, and co-workers to fill us up and make us feel loved. We look outside ourselves for validation that we matter. The path to self-love begins with creating internal boundaries that give us space to be our own best friend, lover, and hero.

There are several signs that you need better internal boundaries. People-pleasing is a big sign and the most common sign. This is when you give and give to others with the expectation that others will give to you when you need it. Then when you do not receive that support, you are angry, resentful, or worse depressed.

Another sign you need better internal boundaries is over apologizing for things outside your control. If a friend invites you to a happy hour, you cannot make it due to a job conflict, then you gush with apologies or negotiate a way to make it up to him or her. As you negotiate for forgiveness, you feel a sense of doom and feel that the friendship will end.

A third sign you need to improve your internal boundaries is choosing to spend time with a specific person, group of people, or place that gives you constant anxiety—but you keep going back. Often, your intuition whispers to you that a situation is not good for you through constant anxiety, a sense of dread, or regular body aches and pains.

Once again, the solution to resolving needless angst is developing healthy internal boundaries that wrap you in the warm, safe glow of self-love.

To fall in love with yourself is the first secret to happiness.

– Robert Morley

37: Self-Love: Set Internal Boundaries (Part 2)

Welcome to part 2 of self-love: set internal boundaries.

Happiness is an inside job. In this life, you are responsible for identifying what you need to feel loved, safe, and appreciated. When you stop relying on other people and situations outside your control, you are free to soar.

The first suggestion to setting healthy internal boundaries is knowing your hard limits. Give yourself permission to say "no" and walk away from situations that do not serve you well. Whether is it the friend asking to borrow money, the rude grocery store clerk, or even the crowded shopping mall making you feel a ton of anxiety—you can decide to say "no" and walk away. A tool that works for some, is to have a very elaborate internal dialogue discussing the pros and cons of the uncomfortable person or situation. Pause for a second and think about it. This may sound silly, but nobody can hear you. Nobody can judge you. And no, you are not crazy.

The second step to building internal boundaries is to trust yourself. No matter the day, week, season, you are a person of value and equal to all others. Identify and prioritize your needs. Then, organize your life, literally and figuratively. It could be something as simple as getting a rewards card for your daily coffee break at Starbucks. It could be giving away all the clothes that no longer fit from 10 years ago and hanging your favorite go-to outfits in the closet. Maybe you get a sound machine for a good night's sleep when the neighbor's dog spends the night howling at the moon. You decide what is important and act on it.

An important foundation to self-love is accepting that you have your own thoughts and beliefs independent of others. You have the power to shape these beliefs without needing approval from others. Opinions can inform you of your choices, but someone else does not decide for you. A free tool to use is positive affirmation. Whether you find them on your phone, laptop, or paperback book, there is something out there for every personality. Use affirmations daily, weekly, or every three hours. Your choice.

These are a few suggestions to set internal boundaries based on self-love. There is more to come.

How you love yourself is how you teach others to love you.

– Rupi Kaur

38: Self-Love: Owning Your Power (Part 3)

There are situations outside our control such as flash floods, the money pox outbreak, and political unrest. The concept of owning your power may sound like a difficult mountain to climb. However, awareness of an unhealthy pattern is the first step to change.

Children have a need to be nurtured and to receive modeling of appropriate behavior for success in life. Some begin life with a solid foundation, and some do not. As an adult, you choose your thoughts, words, and actions. You have power. You can own your power. The power comes from within.

Clearly define what you need and want for your current stage in life. Your needs and wants may not be the same as 5 years ago. They may change 10 years from now. Focus on what really matters today will help you have healthy, positive goals for moving forward in work, love, and life.

Identify tools and strategies that will develop the personal hero within. For example, do you need a professional therapist, a support group, self-help book, podcast, journaling, or something completely different?

Learn to be "selfish." As you walk the path to owning your power, the people around you will still pull at you with expectations. The boss may expect you to pull an all-nighter for a last-minute work project. Your friend may still break up with his girlfriend and want to vent for the next month. A great tool to own your power is assertive communication. It is important to learn to say "no" where the other person still feels respected, and you set personal boundaries.

Curious?

Most folks are about as happy as they make up their minds to be.

– Abraham Lincoln

39: Mastering Negative Self-Talk

Life, real life is a series of successes and failures. Sometimes we feel as if we are on top of the mountain. And sometimes, we feel low in the valley. How we talk to ourselves when we are low in the valley determines how quickly we bounce back. No matter the size of your personal circle of family, friends, and co-workers, YOU should be the biggest cheerleader in your life. Always talk to yourself with kindness, compassion, and forgiveness.

What is Negative Self-Talk?

Negative self-talk is a common battle many of us must face from time to time. Negative self-talk is feeling disappointed that we were not perfect in a certain situation. Negative self-talk is thinking in absolutes and extremes. It is believing in terms around "you always" or "you never." Failure is perceived to be a way of life, instead of a temporary, normal setback that happens to all of us from time to time. Negative self-talk can spiral into depression, anxiety, and chronic insomnia if not properly addressed.

How to Beat Negative Self-Talk?

Do not try to stop your thoughts. It is impossible. Acknowledge you have difficult feelings. Try to diagnose why. Replace them with a better alternative.
Are you a planner? If a project fails, figure out how to revise your steps to get better results next time. If a relationship fails, accept your part, and only your part. You have no control over the thoughts and actions of others. What can you learn to do differently with the next companion? If you set a personal goal and fell short, sometimes, just sometimes, it was not meant to be. What is the second-best goal you can obtain?

Are you more spiritual?

Words have power. Replace your negative self-talk with affirmations, mantras, poetry of love. You can find free resources online and collect positive affirmations and quotes that you can say each day. Depending on your faith, every religion has spiritual mantras to connect you to a higher Power. Release yourself from trying to control everything in your life. Listen to motivational podcasts or YouTube videos and simply tap into good feelings as needed, whenever you need it.

Do you like to get physical?

Practice mindfulness, deep breathing, and exercise. Mindfulness is being in the moment and not focusing on the past or the future. You can practice mindfulness through meditation. You might start with just 5 minutes a day. Practice mindful breathing. Appreciate being alive when others have already crossed over. You do not have to be an athlete to appreciate exercise. You can go for a walk outside. Dance to a YouTube video for 5 minutes. You can do some stretching before going to bed. Keep it simple. Allow small accomplishments to replace your negative self-talk.

Believe in yourself. You are braver than you think, more talented than you know, and capable of more than you imagine.

– Roy T. Bennett

40: Unshakeable Confidence

Having unshakeable confidence is the key to navigating a world of inflation, political stances, and civil unrest. Healthy self-confidence helps us step out into the unknown and walk our own unique path. Without some level of confidence, we are defeated before we begin.

What is self-confidence?

Self-confidence is not the same thing as self-esteem. Healthy self-esteem means you place a high value on yourself. You have strong self-worth. You like yourself. Self-confidence is the belief that you can accomplish different goals regardless of your actual skill level.

How do you build self-confidence?

Having unshakeable confidence changes the beliefs you have about yourself, and it takes work. Building and maintaining healthy confidence takes daily practice. You do not just *arrive,* then magically you are done for life.

Step 1: Try things outside your comfort zone

Stepping outside your comfort zone is, as you might expect, uncomfortable. Real confidence is the ability to be comfortable in a variety of situations that would make most people uncomfortable. You can challenge yourself in large and small ways. For example, you might take on a new job or confront someone you usually avoid. Maybe you strike up a conversation with someone new if you are normally shy. Maybe you try a new cuisine at a restaurant. It is more important you regularly challenge your comfort zone in small ways rather than jump off the deep end in major ways.

Step 2: Try a new look

How you dress can affect how other people perceive you, but it can also affect how you perceive yourself. Wearing different clothes can prompt you to think or behave differently. This effect is not just limited to feeling good about yourself. For example, if you want that management job, try wearing a tie from time to time. Look at the part, even if you have not actually been hired. If you want to feel more confident, dress the way a confident version of yourself would.

Step 3: Use powerful body language

Much like how you dress, your posture and body language can affect how you feel about yourself. This might seem smaller, smaller, powerful stances. Great posture can help adjust your frame of mind. When you are closing a deal in business, plant your hands on the table and lean forward. When you are pitching an idea, rest your feet on the table, clasp your hands behind your head, and lean back. Before an interview, plant your feet wide and stretch your arms overhead in a V shape. When talking to your boss, puff out your chest, plant your hands on your hips, and stand with feet hip-width apart.

The first to apologize is the bravest.
The first to forgive is the strongest.
The first to forget is the happiest.

– Unknown

41: Saying "I'm Sorry!"

Sometimes we really screw things up. You are not the victim— you are the one who stirred sh*t up! It is important to know how to give a genuine apology. If you want to repair the relationship, asking for forgiveness is key.

According to relationship experts, *Paired Life*, apologizing to your partner involves more than just saying "I'm sorry." There are many things you can do— from taking responsibility for your actions to resisting the urge to pull out the so-called "scorecard" that will make your apology come across sincerely.

How to Give a Sincere and Heartfelt Apology
- Avoid using the word "but."
- Do not take your partner's forgiveness for granted. Ask—but do not demand—that you be forgiven for your mistake.
- Do not blame your partner for how you behaved. Take responsibility for the hurtful things that you said and did.
- Express your gratitude for your partner's patience.
- Choose words and phrases that are soft, gentle, and sincere, but make sure they sound like things you would actually say. Do not try to be someone else when you apologize for your blunder. Being fake is the worst way to say sorry!
- If you are writing a note to say sorry to your lover, put some thought into your writing materials. A handwritten card is far more personal and sincere than a message sent by text or email.

An apology is the superglue of life. It can repair just about anything. We all make mistakes. Admitting your mistakes and making repairs are the marks of maturity. Unless you are rich and famous, you do not have endless friends and lovers. Learn to give a heartfelt apology.

Gratitude turns what we have into enough.

– Maya Angelou

42: The Power of Gratitude

Practicing gratitude is an extremely effective tool for coping during a crisis. Regularly expressing thankfulness also helps you ride the peaks and valleys in life. There are different ways to express feeling blessed. Gratitude journaling will deliver most if not all the benefits.

The dictionary definition of gratitude states: "the quality of being thankful; readiness to show appreciation for and to return kindness." Simply put, whether you are having a good day or bad day, you find a few things to appreciate in your life. You can be thankful that you wake up in good health when others may be struggling. You can be thankful for having food in the refrigerator when others do without. You can be grateful for having access to family through technology when others live in a drop zone.

Journaling every day is a great habit to start. Expressing gratitude through writing has a wealth of benefits. For example, you may experience the following:
1. Boost your long-term well-being, encouraging exercise, reducing physical pain and symptoms, and increasing both length and quality of sleep
2. Increase your optimism and, indirectly, your happiness and health
3. Make you friendlier, more open, and expand your social support network
4. Help you make progress toward your goals

Gratitude journaling requires little resources. There are free mobile apps where you can log your daily appreciation. Every day pick three things you are grateful for – no matter how large or small. Express what you are grateful for and the "because." Adding the why is important and sparks your "feel good" brain center.

I am no bird; and no net ensnares me; I am a free human being with an independent will.

–Charlotte Brontë

43: Love and Independence

She loves me. She loves me not. He loves me. He loves me not.

Love of self eliminates the need to be approved and accepted by others. You can just BE.

What is self-love? When you love yourself, you accept your strengths and weakness. You can always strive to be better, but perfection is an illusion. Sometimes all hell breaks loose, and things get messy. But that is part of life. You laugh it off. You cry and get tissue. You get mad and scream in your car. But then you bounce back and keep at it.

Having love of self also means you understand that the world does not owe you anything. It is not another person's responsibility to make you happy or entertain you. Do not expect someone to make radical changes to accommodate you and your desires. You have the power to obtain your own happiness.

How do you develop self-love? At some point, you take a hard look at who you are in life. What makes you strong? What makes you falter? Then balance the line between what is healthy and excessive. Setting boundaries around difficult people and tricky situations is important. Some challenges in life are necessary, but if a person or situation regularly upsets you, cut them out.

Create the opportunity for daily pleasures. You can love dark chocolate and have a bite after dinner. But you might not want to eat a whole bar every day, indefinitely. Try the decadent hand cream that comes in the tiny jar. You might not use it every day, all day long, but maybe slather it on before bed. See the sunrise on a Sunday morning. However, it may not be something you can commit to every day with work, family, etc. Start small, carve out the time, enjoy daily pleasures.

Trust takes years to build, seconds to break, and forever to repair.

– Unknown

44: Building Trust, Part 1

Trust and communication are the key to any successful relationship. When you first start dating someone, you want to bring your A game. You want to appear attractive, successful, confident, and more. Never, never start a relationship with deception and expect to be forgiven later.

Here are a few tips and strategies to build trust in a relationship according to *Positive Psychology:*

Be true to your word and follow through with your actions
The point of building trust is for others to believe what you say. Keep in mind, however, that building trust requires not only keeping the promises you make but also not making promises you are unable to keep.

Learn how to communicate effectively with others
Poor communication is a major reason why relationships break down. Effective communication includes being clear about what you have or have not committed to and what has been agreed upon. Building trust is not without risk. It involves allowing both you and others to take risks to prove trustworthiness.

Remind yourself that it takes time to build and earn trust
Building trust is a daily commitment. Do not make the mistake of expecting too much too soon. To build trust, first take small steps and take on small commitments and then, as trust grows, you will be more at ease with making and accepting bigger commitments. Put trust in, and you will generally get trust in return.

Take time to make decisions and think before acting too quickly
Only make commitments that you are happy to agree with. Have the courage to say "no," even when it disappoints someone. If you agree to something and cannot follow through, everyone involved is worse off.

Value the relationships that you have—and do not take them for granted
Trust often results from consistency. We tend to have the most trust in people who are there for us consistently through good times and bad. Regularly showing someone that you are there for them is an effective way to build trust.

Pain changes people, it makes them trust less, overthink more, and shut people out.

– Unknown

45: Building Trust, Part 2

Unless you meet and marry your soul mate during high school, chances are you have had failed relationship and been hurt. Some people bounce back more easily from disappointing relationships than others. If you are dating a good but overly cautious person, give it time. Do not take the walls personally. Do not expect the person to tell you their whole life story on the first or second date. More than likely, you are dealing with someone who has been deeply hurt in love, is willing to try again, but needs time. Be patient.

Here are more tips and strategies to build trust in a relationship:

Always be honest
The message you convey should always, always be the truth. If you are caught telling a lie, no matter how small, your trustworthiness will be diminished.

Help people whenever you can
Helping another person, even if it provides no benefit to you, builds trust. Authentic kindness helps to build trust.

Do not hide your feelings
Being open about your emotions is often an effective way to build trust. Furthermore, if people know that you care, they are more likely to trust you. Emotional intelligence plays a role in building trust. Acknowledging your feelings, learning the lessons that prevail, and taking productive action means that you will not deny reality—this is the key to building trust.

Always do what you believe to be right
Doing something purely for approval means sacrificing your own values and beliefs. This decreases trust in yourself, your values, and your beliefs. Always doing what you believe is right, even when others disagree, will lead others to respect your honesty. Interestingly, when building trust, you must be willing to upset others on occasion. People tend not to trust those who simply say whatever they think others want to hear.

Admit your mistakes
When you attempt to hide your mistakes, people know that you are dishonest. By being open, you show your vulnerable side, and this helps build trust with other people. This is because they perceive you to be more like everyone makes mistakes. When all that a person sees is the "perfection" you project, they likely will not trust you.

Relationships don't last because of the good times; they last because the hard times were handled with love and care.

– Author Unknown

46: *Grow Your Emotional IQ and Grow Your Love IQ*

Love relationships are not without certain challenges and obstacles. How you handle the challenging times determines the longevity of your relationship. Nobody is perfect. Your partner needs to know that even when he or she makes a mistake, you will still have love and trust.

To grow your emotional IQ and in turn have more love in your life, try the following tips and strategies:

Observe how you react to people. Do you rush to judgment before you know all the facts? Do you stereotype? Look honestly at how you think and interact with other people. Try to put yourself in their place and be more open and accept their perspectives and needs.

Look at your work environment. Do you seek attention for your accomplishments? Humility can be a wonderful quality, and it does not mean that you are shy or lack self-confidence. When you practice humility, you say that you know what you did, and you can be quietly confident about it. Give others a chance to shine – put the focus on them, and do not worry too much about getting praise for yourself.

Do a self-evaluation. What are your weaknesses? Are you willing to accept that you are not perfect and that you could work on some areas to make yourself a better person? Have the courage to look at yourself honestly – it can change your life.

Examine how you react to stressful situations. Do you become upset every time there is a delay or something does not happen the way you want? Do you blame others or become angry at them, even when it is not their fault? The ability to stay calm and in control in tricky situations is highly valued – in the business world and outside it. Keep your emotions under control when things go wrong.

Take responsibility for your actions. If you hurt someone's feelings, apologize directly – do not ignore what you did or avoid the person. People are usually more willing to forgive and forget if you make an honest attempt to make things right.

Examine how your actions will affect others – before you take those actions. If your decision impacts others, put yourself in their place. How will they feel if you do this? Would you want that experience? If you must take the action, how can you help others deal with the effects?

To find yourself, think for yourself.

– Socrates

47: Team Cooperation vs Herd Mentality

Most employers today will tell you that they want employees that are team players. If you have been in the workforce for any length of time, you know it is important to go along to get along. *We've all gotta eat.* However, there is a difference between being a team player and having a herd mentality in unethical situations.

What is herd mentality?
The Webster definition of herd mentality is "the tendency of the people in a group to think and behave in ways that conform with others in the group rather than as individuals." In simpler terms, you do what everybody else does even when it is simply, *stoopid.* If you work in a restaurant and your team leader says spit in the bad customer's drink, you do it to fit in, even though it is the wrong thing to do. If you are on a committee at work and the team leader is threatened and intimidated by the new hire, you withhold important company updates from the new hire, so they struggle to succeed. If you are working on a management project and the team leader has personal issues and is missing meetings, you slow down production, miss deadlines, to fit in with the weakest link and be liked.

Herd mentality skews towards the negative. Difficult personalities in the workplace have some charisma and the ability to lead others into misfortune. Watch out for this! If you find that your morality is constantly challenged in work situations, it might not be a good fit for you. Typically, you know if a job is a good fit in the first 90 days. Keep your eyes open for company snake charmers.

What is being a team player?
Being a team player is understanding the company's vision and goals to make positive strives to support the bigger picture. When the company wins, you win! Here are some strategies to be the right team player:

- Understand your role
- Embrace positive collaboration
- Hold yourself accountable
- Commit to the team
- Be flexible
- Be optimistic
- Back up goals with action

If you are working for a company that is the right fit, you embrace the challenge of supporting great people with healthy goals and values.

Strength does not come from winning. Your struggles develop your strengths. When you go through hardships and decide not to surrender, that is strength.

— Mohandas Gandhi

48: The Resilient Warrior

The most basic definition of resilience is the ability to recover from or adjust easily to misfortune or change. You must imagine yourself to be a rubber band to navigate in this world of pandemics, political stances, and civil unrest. You stretch. You bounce back. No matter what, your strength lies in your ability to recover from stresses and challenges.

There are multiple benefits to becoming a resilient warrior:

- Improved relationships
- Improved coping when we experience emotional disruptions
- Improved working memory
- Improved immune system function and sleep
- Decreased depressive symptoms & increased emotional well-being

There are great and simple ways to build resilience that are approved by the American Psychological Association.

- Make connections. Good relationships with close family members, friends, or others are important.
- Accept help and support from those who care about you and will listen to you strengthens resilience.
- Some people find that being active in civic groups, faith-based organizations, or other local groups provides social support and can help with reclaiming hope. Assisting others in their time of need can also benefit the helper.
- Avoid seeing crises as insurmountable problems. You cannot change the fact that highly stressful events happen, but you can change how you interpret and respond to these events.
- Accept that change is a part of living. Certain goals may no longer be attainable as a result of adverse situations. Accepting circumstances that cannot be changed can help you focus on circumstances that you can alter.
- Move toward your goals. Develop some realistic goals. Do something regularly -- even if it seems like a small accomplishment -- that enables you to move toward your goals. Instead of focusing on tasks that seem unachievable.
- Take care of yourself. Pay attention to your own needs and feelings. Engage in activities that you enjoy and find relaxing. Exercise regularly.
- Additional ways of strengthening resilience may be helpful. For example, some people write about their deepest thoughts and feelings

related to trauma or other stressful events in their life. Meditation and spiritual practices help some people build connections and restore hope.

No matter your circumstances, imagine yourself to be that rubber band. Face challenges head on, be willing to stretch, but do not let it break you. Build a positive support team and be willing to help others.

Every silver lining has a cloud.

—Mary Kay Ash

49: The Silver Lining

Calm and clear your mind. Consider your struggles and successes. When you wake up in the morning do you choose to try again? Or just lay in bed defeated? If you choose to try again, that is the silver lining. Write it down. Hold on to it. Keeping a journal can help you commit to seeing the positive side of life and set goals. Your ideas to overcome challenges may be fuzzy at first. However, the process of writing and rewriting can create a laser focus.

Try to set aside fifteen to twenty minutes a day to journal. Review your goals, think about your options to accomplish tasks, then prioritize. If possible, write around the same time each day.

Journaling allows you to record progress. If you have struggles or setbacks, you can record it in your journal. Then you work through to solutions and see the silver lining. If you ever have a difficult day, you can take out your journal and review the progress you have made.

Writing is an opportunity to explore your feelings and address barriers to your progress. Sometimes we are our own worst enemy. We do not believe in ourselves. We let doubts hold us back. We have negative self-talk. Journal all the negative feelings. Release them. Then plan realistic next steps to achieving your important goals.

Finally, journaling can help you keep the ball rolling. Vent the difficult emotions. Identify the silver lining. Create a to do list. Each day before you close the journal, give yourself an assignment. Choose something you can accomplish in the next 24-48 hours.

When dealing with people, remember you are not dealing with creatures of logic, but with creatures of emotion.

– Dale Carnegie

50: The Power of Words

Words have power. You can build bridges or destroy with the power of words. Before you speak to others, ask yourself—Is it true? Is it kind? Is it inspiring? Is it necessary? Be a role model of integrity, charisma, and good emotional IQ. Overtime, you will draw in like minds and hopefully build a community where people motivate and encourage others to be their best.

Avoid pitfalls

In the workplace, communities, and families, we have plenty of Debbie Downers. Criticizing and complaining is easy. Office gossip is often co-workers using their free time to claim victimhood and complain and complain about the people around them. Scientific studies show that human beings skew negative. We take small disappointments and make them super large to avoid danger in the future. Do not join in spirals of spoken negativity!

How to give positive feedback

If given the opportunity to give feedback, take the time to consider the project or situation being discussed. Share two positives and one area of concern. People are easily overwhelmed and discouraged from the critique of others. A person has the focus and energy to address one to two areas of improvement. If you are in a management position, you want to motivate your team to do better and not demoralize them into mediocrity.

How to connect emotionally with others

Depending on the circumstances, when you meet new people, you have to consider the environment and the temperament of this stranger. It is much better to discuss universal topics that anyone can speak on. Some examples include the weather, good food at an event, inspiring presentations, and even music hits. Do not require a stranger to share their sensitive personal characteristics like marital status, child status, age, etc. for your entertainment. If there is something personal you with to know in good faith, try telling a story about yourself first. If the other person feels comfortable, he or she will share. If they do not, it is nothing personal.

Finally, give it time. You never know what someone else is going through. And sometimes people are simply preoccupied with different issues in their world. Not to stereotype, but some private people take a little more time to warm up and connect. Private people, sometimes labeled introverts, often have the most genuine, soft hearts and they protect it.

ABOUT THE AUTHOR

RL Collins is a Virginia native. She has been writing since she was in middle school. She spent a lot of time outside in nature wandering with her dog. Together, they observed life on land, in water, and in the air. By night, she would write about the grand adventures of ordinary people. "Blood Magic" is her first published paranormal romance and suspense book series. "The Hard Work of Happiness: 50 Life Lessons" is the third installment in her motivational and self-help book series, "The Life and Times of Indigo Stone."